The Poets of New England

Underground Writers Association 2018

UNDERGROUND WRITERS ASSOCIATION

Cover Design by Joel Carpenter
Interior Design by Joel Carpenter
Editors: Valeri Beers, Josh Nicolaisen

Proof read by: Joel Carpenter

Underground Writers Association
Portland, Maine

Support Indie Publishing
facebook.com/undergroundwritersassociation

ISBN-13: 978-1727627930
ISBN-10: 1727627938

CONTENTS

Lynne Schmidt
How Forever Feels

I am holding on to a string
That has been stretched so tight
It is only a matter of time before it snaps apart
Like a rubber band,
And strikes the hand that is still refusing to let go.
It is too hard to pry apart these fingers
Release this grasp
Because the last thread that is here
Bound me from this place to home,
To my sister's apartment,
To the first place I ever really knew myself and began to sew my insides
back together.
I understood how the world worked then,
How gravity kept me safe,
Even in those moments where I scraped my knees.
I knew how the stars hung,
Why the tides went out and came back
To the beaches even when skin burns in sunlight.
I knew then that happiness tasted like salt stained lips,
And fingertips that interlocked beside fire.
And while I cling to this,
What's right here, right now,
Like a child and their safety blanket that has been through eighteen too
many washes,
I know this piece is a ticking alarm
Or bomb
That will burst apart my chest.
And there will be yet another void,
Another hole,
Gap,
Puzzle piece that makes the larger picture haunted with ghosts because it
can't be complete.
And so I cling onto this piece,
Wood from a sinking ship,
Because the only thing I know
Is the permanence of impermanence.
And how empty forever feels.

Lynne Schmidt
Defining Our Relationship

I tried you on the tip of my tongue,
First, as Your Name--
how you introduced yourself the night we met.
As Boyfriend,
The name you refuse to know with me.
As Partner
A name we whisper in the night
When the lights are off
And the drinks become too much
And I learn to keep my hands to myself.
Until
You lean over and moan my name.
But the name you curl
With your tongue against mine
Is Friend.
But after years of dissecting friendships like frogs
On a seventh grade science table
I have learned that friends sit through the sad
And don't leave you at a table
Like yesterday's picnic.

Lynne Schmidt
The Ashes of You and Me

You're supposed to be better than me,
The gold standard to which all beings strive
And point at, marveling, "Don't you
Want to be this someday?"
You're supposed to be the one
Who cleans my wounds after I licked them raw
Who soothes the fire in me
Because you're water
And I am eating away entire forests
And burning bridges made of concrete.
Because you were the one,
To encase the world in bubble wrap,
And hold doors closed when I wanted to jump.
You were supposed to be the one to show up.
Not strike a match
And drop it on the ground under me.
Because I always thought it was
Cement and stable,
Not string, and sticks and dead leaves.
I guess that's the thing about gold standards,
Most of them shine like stars
But are really dollar store paint.

Rachel Maher
Interior Clarity

The wind washes the fog away
Today it's not my friend
Rather, I enjoyed the closeness
Confined to near-sighted news
Alone, at least I thought
If I believed what my eyes told me
Not my heart.
Its seeping softness
Drove me seeking solace
Inside
Not outside where the glare
Caught me off guard and blinded
Yes, inside,
Among the milkweed feathers
Of imaginings and inspirations
Within the white-clouds-come-near
And quiet whispers secrets
To my soul

Rachel Maher
November Skies

November arrived the other day
Backlit by the Beaver Moon
As truth fell on me softly
The Pioneer Woman had gone

Leaving quietly, so as not to stir
Me sleeping,
My bed a den
Of pillows and dreamers

The empty space
Left my mind to fill as the storehouse
For the coming winter,
The winter of my life

I felt the loss
Before I knew; and yet I knew,
As scrips and scraps flowed through my hands
Into those of another craftier than I

Younger, too, as in springtime
Or even summer
Strong ones who carry wood
And water for the thirsty

My days show narrow
As the grey clouds layered behind
Branches laid bare
Who look beyond November skies

Crosby Girón
Verses girl, verses

I

You throb within me
And you run through my spaces

You laugh and my milky nerves explode
Soft petals touch me
With the clouds' hands

You laugh and run cheekily
All of the lights melt amid the dance
They give off sparks over my head...
The birds that fled from my banishment,
which you know nothing of yet

Your embrace has the antidote

For my laughter and joy
Your mouth contains the excesses
You have absences in your hands
Your youthfulness and your sap
Your bright life, the longing for Natalia
Your wildness

II

You will live in an untidy garden
But you have me as casual water
You leap in your throbbing wildness
Look at me in your dreams
Touch me during our moments

Tenderness and peace that we have: out of rot!

Come to me at night as you did before
To sleep in my arms
I will be alert and half-asleep
A bird will be waiting for you
Hiding among little kisses

Like flower buds with little faces

Come to me at night as you did before
And awake me from this pain
Of not sleeping with you

I want to breathe happily your innocent dreams
And to receive, smiling, the awakenings
That were stolen from us
By the terrible and bloody break-up
Caused by a lie...

You will live for some time in an untidy garden
But you have me forever, you have me forever!

III

Last night I chewed an ancestral fear
And I suddenly remembered you
And memory brought me close to your eyes

You had a flower in your hand
And you inhaled the aroma
Of waterless lagoons

When I woke up I knew I was waiting for you
When I woke up I knew you wouldn't come and I cried

Since then every night
Survived the snakes
The spiders and their nests
The beautiful dark streets
So sinister with their concrete and dirty water

Close to uncertainty
I build my kisses and my looks
That will seep in from the distance
And will pierce envy

You are what I have
And what I don't have

All of my flowers
All of my pistils
Blossom for you:

Don't let them rot!

IV

The years in my dead eyes
Have gone
And you being the daughter
of banishment or a woman who
gets up more and more
You open your eyes
To see the world
Without thinking of a path
That comes from me and leads to your eyes
All of those hours of silence from your lips
Come to rest
And you know that

The tears from your childish games
Fall onto the toys
That I can't choose for you

The glass in your windows
Reflect light, we won't use them to cry together
My eyes won't always see
The doors you open to look at the street

But wherever you take your happiness
You will find that winter bird that squawks
Imagining how you frolic
You will watch my longing fly

Girl of nights so joyful
That you will never want to sleep
Every blood flow always vibrates
In millenary and rough, sad distances

There are no gardens in the distance
But I'm dancing with your flowers!

V

Your other companies drag me
To unfortunate dark places

But that morning lit your voice
It merged with my rare crepitant nerves

That sweet morning when you said you loved me
With the sweet vibrations of your voice
The infinite and lost melody
Of these hard years
Came to stay for a long time
Like a dream
in which I beautifully sculpt your smile

That's why the others who share your company don't know
And this will be our secret
Like that tear we shed in the dark
And dried in silence.

Julie A. Dickson
Metaphor City

Down the cobbled streets,
striding at a right lively clip
a humorous quip dancing
in my head, begged me to stop,
instead of getting along
to a destination, I forgot
where I was going and stood,
perused surroundings then,
couldn't remember
where this street led
When I was still, I heard
city birds, maybe pigeons
or mourning doves cooing,
and while I was brooding,
thinking of my next action,
my reaction was to leave
the metaphor city, after all,
more of a suburban gal –
what do I want of bustle
and crowds, noisy and loud
when I could see trees,
not rooted in planters
on street corners, no leaves
Fields are better to view,
and a lake or pond
with regrets or a few
ducks yakking their find,
my mind clear of cluttery
taxi stands, better a stand
of birch trees or maple
in spring, with spinners
descending to my feet,
on soft ground, not concrete
of city street,
where I stand now

Julie A. Dickson
Kayaking - Saco River

Swirling waters,
currents drive against
my tiny vessel
even as I back-paddle
pulls me far to the bank,
threat of exposed
tree roots, eroded
with the constant flow
of swift river wide
As branches blow
and leaves above
no tide to ebb
formations loom
silhouettes shadow
the evening sky
Just ahead, a wolf?
No, just a log;
I drift along aloof,
lost in the currents
of thoughts, floating
through a timeless
memory in the making

Michael Koch

One Drop ...
one drop ...
of sunshine
of effort
of warmth
of faith
of care
of kindness
of belief
of love
of laughter
of compassion
of help
of understanding
of will
of courage
of life
of water
one pine needle.

Photo by Michael Koch

Geoffrey Blanchette
The Best That We Can Do

We haven't done a lot of things together
We don't have any places of our own
We don't have a whole lot of things in common
But neither of us wants to be alone

I guess that we should really be together
Although I really don't have any clue
What's gonna keep us going too much longer
Maybe we're just the best that we can do

We don't have mutual friends to argue over
On quiet nights alone, we can't decide
Whether we'd rather drink or watch a movie
But that's the kind of problem we abide

My cat thinks you're an interloper
Your dog thinks I'm its new squeaky toy
The birds will just ignore us altogether
The rats will watch us all and squeal with joy

I guess that we're just meant to be together
Though you're not quite the one I thought I knew
Maybe with time we'll settle for each other
And know that we're the best that we can do

I can't imagine life forever with you
I can't imagine love forevermore
But you say life is kind of dull without me
And in the end I'd hate to see you bored

It looks like we will always be together
And every day I realize anew
We never really had a thing in common
Except we were the best that we could do

Gloria Monaghan
The Meadow

The red stable horse in
the meadow of darkened lavender
brings forth a deeper red
of the rose blossoms
in the early fall.

In the forest in the pine overhead
Michigan dirt and rust smell
of the creek

the bone of archers in the ankles
inherited
running through grass,
Orpheus in the shadow.

His sweet kisses light the way.
A smile on his face through
the branches of the willow.
Coming toward you
his hand outstretched.

It is a game this coming and going
running away and laughing
hiding behind the tree,
he has your wrist
presses you against the tree.

His sweet kisses light the way.
His smile fades slowly into
sadness for what is lost.

Don't tell me about death; my child
I don't want to hear it.

David Thomas Jr.
I MET A DAYDREAM

I met a daydream
She stood about a little less tall than me
She had pale skin
And hair the color of the speed of light

She took perfect photographs
And she spoke in a tone that made you listen
But like listen because she played symphonies with her words
She spewed pure soul
A New York runaway from the ocean state
Locked in a city scape that makes her sick
I know her well
You see
I once walked where the wild things are.
They exist.
They are bare foot with muddy feet and they are beautiful.
Their laughs are melodies played from sun ray strings.
They dance and they drink and they spit and they love.
They twirl in the forest like fairies
If I'm lucky, I'll walk there again someday.
With her and we'll create everything we've ever thought
Uncensored
Just like them

Faster than the speed of her hair
I'm pushing for a resolution to a broken heart
I have no cure for
And
I've found her
And whether this is here or there
Or neither nor
My heart belongs to her in the fall
I trust her with my shaky leaves
She's a visible breathe on a crisp morning coming from my lungs that's
convincing my brain
I'm still alive

I met a daydream
She punched me with her poetry and I fell into her womanly wisdom

For she knows all
She was the moon in pure day light.
The sun at midnight.
A walking talking eclipse 24/7.
I am barely a blade of fucking grass.
She was a glass of wine rolled in diamonds and I wanted to get High off of
her
I looked forward to withdrawing off of her
The shakes and sweats remind me of the first time I thought about her
nude.

In my noir jazz music life feature film I was sad
And her soul illuminated it like a Technicolor blast
I watched her, knee deep in a pond, raising her arms to the sun like a
beautiful plant sprouting from the
ground under the water to the sky begging for air and life.
She was my Mother Nature
She was my Father Time
Because when I'm around her I have no past.
I don't care about my future I'm just present, in her presence.

The clocks on my walls cry because I haven't checked them since I met her,
they don't even move their
hands anymore.
One even grew feet and tried to dance for me just to catch my attention
I closed my eyes
It's the middle of the afternoon, I'm high, and I just met a daydream
I hope she haunts me
I hope she's also my night dreams because
I welcome waking up in a cold sweat because of you
I can't wait to toss and turn
Because every time my eyes close I see you
A promise of tomorrow with fairy wings dancing happily to the blues.
And when I think of you moving I move too.

I met a day dream
And I don't want to wake up from her
So please self
Don't show her you're a nightmare

Brandy Garcia
We Must Overcome

Someday

Women won't live in fear

Till this day we must empower one another

Someday

Women won't be silenced

Till this day we must speak for those who can not

Someday

Women won't be objectified

Till this day we must demand change

Someday

Our daughters and granddaughters will rise above

Till this day we must fight for equality

Someday

Nicole Jean Turner
The Astronaut

This is the third interstellar bar this week.
On a pioneer's never finished journey,
a neon hall behind a blue reflection;
he's drinking an oil slick again.

This is just another surface to sit, take off the helmet for a bit,
strain the lungs on some fresh thin air, here, we find the astronaut
in his natural habitat. A pit stop
somewhere on the way to sector whatever
the destination never matters.
He won't be staying long.

He gets high on the atmosphere and strung out on change,
he hangs at the rail just long enough
to be overwhelmed by epinephrine
endorphins, the closest thing he can remember
to how it felt to be warm without the suit.

This astronaut, he drinks black ice and chews lime tonic,
befriends for the night the same type of Martian
from the space bar before, always some regular.
He's jealous of their commitments, telling them,
how lucky to have a name and be wanted
in the place they're most comfortable and understood.

This astronaut, he lives a dream,
charts unseen galaxies,
but can't find the gravity to stay or say;
how sad the heart that beats
thick and full in a body by itself.

He carries on into the glitter searching
for a black hole to fall into, or someone
with more

than just a spare oxygen tank, someone
who'll look at him the way Galileo looked to the moon.

Nicole Jean Turner
Common Grounds

Back home on the east coast,
friends poke fun at the months I've spent
overspending on pour-overs and latte art.
Artisan coffee has become the cliché hobby
I kill time with on my stays in Portland, Oregon.
It speeds things up.
I've refined my palate to pick up notes
of strawberries in Ethiopian roasts
or chocolate in Peruvian espresso.
Even still, when I go home I drink Dunks
just for the sake of being able. Just for
the way the R falls away in ordering a regular
and my voice sounds familiar again.
Out in Oregon, I sit alone
in cafés sipping until I shake
writing home love poems about the snow
I've hardly touched all winter; I admit to missing her.
I admit the life of a transient was never brewed right for me,
I order an iced coffee and daydream out the window
hopeful to return in time for the turning leaves.
Hyper aware from the caffeine how loud the steamer
and clinking porcelain, but at least the rumble of conversation
creates an illusion of company.

Chris LaMay-West
Memories of an Antique Pocket Watch

Someone says "Antique Pocket Watch"

and oblique recollection rises up
of sitting in Aunt Pat's living room
after Grandpa's death
sorting through dusty boxes,
unearthing pock-marked remains of his past:
Rusted harmonica
Yellowed train tickets
Faded pictures of past infidelities
stretching from Little Rock to Los Angeles
And the watch,
nearly pristine,
its gold slightly brassy with age,
almost the same color as my cousin Amanda's
dyed hair
Improper yearning rolls to the surface

at decade-old thoughts of her,
white whale of unattainable desire,
consanguinity an obvious bar
to forward motion,
add to that she's a recovering meth addict,
and I've found over the years
that the recovery girls just don't groove on me,
despite a sterling pedigree

Though there are reasons to doubt this:
Courtney, Kristy, Sarah,
and Dear Roz, who seemed surly and guarded
until that night at her party
when she joked about me picking her up
(physically, she meant, by the waist)
and in the round of parting hugs
after a meeting one night,
even kissed me on the neck
I didn't know what to do with that,
have never known what to do with these things,

my reserve more deadly to me than smallpox

Awkward stilted memories of chances untaken,
only partially faded by the mercy of time,
stretch all the way back
to third grade recess chase and run
I had a pocket watch then too,
don't even remember who gave it to me,
lost now, like so many things from those days
The Pocket Guide to Stars and Planets
fell from my backpack
down the side of a grassy hill
I found it weeks later
dry despite rain and fog in-between,
the pages wrinkled,
covered in delicate spidery webs of mold

Other things were lost in the jumbled terrain of the closet,
the dark swath under the bed,
and on the overstuffed bookshelf,
where a red leather-covered Bible,
whose brightly colored maps I still covet
disappeared when the room became Josh's
after I went to college
My brother Josh lost now too
drowned in a creek at 29
while out on bail

And so it goes,
with the star guide,
nettling memories of women past,
my brother:

Some things you get back,
but they're not the same.
Some, though lost,
remain in memory that cannot be shorn.
And some

are just gone.

Joshua Maxson
Sex and death

I met love in my dreams. It was two blondes. They were one. They were
sexual, and I was with them. the lust was palpable, curvy, white hot.
Pumping and thick on dark silk sheets. Buried in nipples and lips. It was
wet and fantastic, slipping into pure ecstasy my thoughts were numb. My
heart pumped in my face, they swallowed me whole. Fireworks in my toes
and knees and elbows. I awoke in an odd fog, my appendage half filled with
blood, my head filled with longing. I fell from the stars. It faded over time,
back into my black and white, grungy sullen mud life. I looked in the
mirror. My belly was disgusting, my jowls embarrassing, hair on my
shoulders, bags under my eyes. I wheezed tying my shoes.

I met love again two nights later. She was Japanese and small. Jet black
straight hair fell down to her cheeks, impeccable, glowing. She was brilliant.
Her breast flesh was like god. Skin like flawless chocolate. I felt with my
hand her soft thigh, heat radiating from above onto my skin. I overflowed
with desire, just short of seizure, starved. She leaned away, was cruel,
domineering, unimpressed, sick of life, too intense.

All the beauty in the world, packed too tight. She wanted to kill me. I tried
to plead with her, sitting across from her Indian style, pathetic. Her eyes
were beautiful hard steel. Her body perfect. Radiating death and secrets.
Worthy of worship. She grasped my soul's riddles and didn't care.

She saw through me, I was empty and boring, nothing to offer. She was
offended. I was disgusting. She picked up a Gun and I ran. She shot at me
but missed. I kept running. I knew she rose and came after me, naked, but I
didn't look back. People were screaming for me to keep going, I was
running upstairs and through doors trying to find an exit, my heart
scorching ready to pop, blinding sweat beads like foggy windows, the light
nimble
patter of deaths footsteps behind me.

All the while wanting to turn back, measuring the risk of wanting to just be
with her one more time, to see her, the last thing before I die. But I kept
running. I haven't seen her since. I wanted to be sick with her, dead inside
with her, but I wasn't good enough. I was too weak. I was too old. It was
too late.

Elsbeth Willis

Stratham, NH

Elsbeth Willis
Summer Showers

On the cusp of a thunderstorm
I watch as the delicate robins
Rush to their makeshift homes,
Between a shaft of metal
and the electric lines.
The trees sway violently
and I'm reminded of your lips
reluctantly curled in a
Grin, baring
gritted teeth and
the shame you felt in missing me.

I wonder what the echo's like
in a thundercloud.
How loud does it clap?
Would it shake my bones?
Or rattle my teeth,
like yours did
when you jumped in the sea
in late September
only to join me?
Because, you said,
You loved me
that
much.
I can't see the rain at first,
    Only the leaves,
            bending to its weight.

And as the sky lightens to your
favorite shade of gangrene,
The earth,
drowning in its own grime,
and sunken to stone;
I hear the melody of you
With each lowly, falling drop.
With the harsh splatter
of resistance,
against a hardened world.

Elsbeth Willis
Follow Me

Follow me down
this path of crushed almond;
my peppered steps
move me two by two
to you, to you.

Breathe me in,
a seeping, stolen eyeflash
of wildfire,
inflaming those lungs
filled with mungdung,
and incessant smokeache.

Sip me slight,
for there's not much left.
Drought after endless drought—
a barren-cursed little trough,
of sundrops Horus forgot.

Tourmaline
I bit and sucked
your tourmaline blood,
seeping deeply within
the fallen pretences
and hallowed expectations.

Infused, bemused
following the (slightly) confused
but clarity of edge—
the tangibilitiy of the desperate curve of your back-
-handed simply wonderous pain,
that I lapped up fervently.
I've never had such fire,
such licking flames
of succulent virgin lands
plundered,
rightly so;
and so,

You:
 with your tainted gaze
ever searching for something
to tear
and rip
and delve into.
I will be your well—
Wishers never suited me as such,
I find beneath their burning brush
nothing but mundane ash.

And so,
          you,
with your deeply embered
call to remember
that what we are
and what we make
and respect
and destroy
and rebuild,
is life disguised as death.

And so,
          I
indulge in the night-time waking,
the fused forsaking
of all I thought I knew
before,
well,
you.

Elsbeth Willis
Porto

A shock of that medieval gait
Iron clad and shut tight behind
our failed visit to this church or that.
Wandering slyly
Sphinx-like in our mysterious gaze
across the Douro
Avoiding eyes but
touching hands
'Because...
Well...Vacation'
he says
slipping his hands down my spine
I say, 'that's fine'
Because...
Well...Temporarity.
But it's not-
Tid in the stomachways.
It churns at the sight of you,
Not in the good way too,
It swivels and slights
always threatening, threatening, threatening
to give up on lunch.

But I guess,
that's all to rest,
because four more days
And you're a stranger again.
Not this succubus sprite
trying to bask in my light,
Not some peeved preacher's son
desperately adopting what I've done,
And not some Disneyland duo,
or too sweetly caricaturized lovers,
But a boy;
and a girl,
Too hurt by this world to admit that
sometimes, it's not where you go
but who you're with
that can ruin the trip.

Elsbeth Willis
Reflections on Prisoner 407

The fear was clear;
These terrified beings
with tags stapled
to their ears,
Plead for remorse.

407,
407,
Do you remember me?
I saw you speeding down 93
locked behind
the fear and hate of man.
You begged me,
and this I know;
I felt your mourning,
I felt your despair.

Oh 407,
I never saw a look like yours
Of which haunted my bones
for miles
and
miles
and
miles.

Dearest 407,
I'm sorry I couldn't save you,
and your friends
crammed into
the back-end of a
glorified garden trailer
hitched to the bumper of
a beat up
piece of shit
sadist pickup truck
going 70 in a 55
not giving a shit
about the lives

he's trapped in his
little hitch.
The dreadful moans and stamps
of souls made of flesh and bone
like you and I.

Like us all.

And goddammit,
maybe you were
bringing them to a new home;
but I'm sure you meant
to slaughter them.
After all,
You only speed,
when the cargo
is disposable.

407 told me so,
with eyes of burdened gold,
weeping.

Elsbeth Willis
Insomnia

Wide eye and wandering
with sleep settled on a separate shore.
Yet, I call once more:
I came for the night keepers,
The soul weepers,
The dream seepers!
And lo! But look!
There is nothing here
But a crooked tree,
Poised east,
And me
with my cursed feet,
Beneath.

Elsbeth Willis
Stacks of Doors

I remember your flat
like an opium den,
the light always lurking
because it knew its unwelcome.

I remember your tiny kitchen,
always untidy.
I remember the smell of stale smoke
and burners slick with oil.

I remember the silent witch next door
casting spells into our moans.
I remember how you ripped me open
and licked the wounds
because you never wanted to hurt me
but show me the rawness of being—
the disproportionate destruction in breath
cartwheeling towards its end
and then
beginning
again.

As if, nothing was
very, very wrong in this world.
As if,
beyond the stacks of doors
you hid your demon behind,
there wasn't a hellish
strength of being.

Art by Wayne Burke

Katrina Thornley
Early Bird

Look closely at firefly wing
See the clock etched in silk membrane
Tick ticks past fast
Blinks become history.
But still the lightning bug burns
It's illumination showing way
For another tomorrow
Until the frog
Snaps it's head and with a tongue flick
The tick tick is gone.

Katie Coleman
Little yellow

little light yellow
inches, slinks up the eave of a house
i've seen a hundred times but never looked at

i have never walked this road at this time of night
i have walked it before
i could walk it right now
i am always walking it, if i want to,
in my head

Caroline Kleiman
Half Empty

Half happy
Half empty
Half laughing
Half sobbing
Half walking
Half standing
Half eating
Half starving
Half here
Half there
Half flying
Half drowning
Half running
Half stumbling
Half dreaming
Half hurting
Half knowing
Half guessing

Fully heartbroken

Michael Morlock
doppleganger

home is where the heartache is stored,
in the attic,
in a tote,
under some old newspapers,
next to the steamer trunk containing the body of the one who caused it
all in the first place.
myself.
a doppleganger, i swear.
but i don't think the courts would see it that way.
our dental records no longer match.
and there's the piece of cloth from my favorite shirt still clutched tight in
a cold rigored fist.
the shirt they are still wearing.
the owls are not what they seem when they burst at the seams.
and the thickest of feather pillows won't silence or drown out the screams.
but they always manage
to take my breath away.

Michele Arcand

Portland, Maine

Michele Arcand
Invisible Voices

I don't exist. And you

You don't exist We don't exist

Traveling down
Two different paths
From two different worlds

But Here we are
Breathing in
the same toxic air
Trying to figure a way out of here... Stumbling around sizing things up Just
trying to maintain

Not getting ourselves to caught up in the game
But debris floats everywhere Through the untold stories
Hidden behind couches and crevices Screaming truths

That refuse to be heard

I don't exist I 'm just a body

A body filling time Filling space Blind down in the trenches On the firing
line

And one by one they drop A new line emerges

They too disappear But not me

Cause I got a hell of a fire
that can remove
that noose from around your neck lift you up from the tracks
I lend you my ear my heart
my very soul
Cause I've got a passion
that drives me to tomorrow
yet I don't exist

And you, you don't exist

Though I see you in the corner

While the sirens fly on by Slumped over, curled up Trembling in a chair
A little cold

And ohhhh so Numb
Talking to the air
And I know the day to day is hard And frustrations at its peak
cause most your time
is just spent waiting
Waiting and waiting and waiting And noise is everywhere waiting Waiting
for relief.....

So roll another smoke
breathe in this toxic air
Just don't let it slip
Or fall down to the ground
Cause one wrong move from you And you'll be gone from here too...

1 by 1 they drop Drifting through the streets

Broke down but needing something more

And anything will do this time Anything
Just feed me
numb my body numb my mind give me something

Anything
And If you do
I swear to fucking god
I'll give you something more Cause I don't exist
You don't see Me
I'm broken
in the corner
Been beaten to my core
And all I hear you say
When I come stumbling
to your door in tears
Is I don't exist

You don't exist We don't exist

But we hear your words hear them loud and clear With a high pitched hint

of sweetness
That Echos through the halls

your actions seem to falter

Leave us flat and wanting more.. And i see you
Sweetly slipping away
All smiles as you walk

these halls
Surrounded by the sounds of outspoken voices Heard no more
Asking for mediocracy asking for complacency while others despair basking
in the glory
Of another success story While we're left
picking up the pieces

Watching loneliness wander the streets again

At night angry and cold

Until numbness takes over

and warmth at any price the call

Yet we're stuck Stomping on truths swallowing our words
Barely breathing
1 2 3 4 ....

Another fallen angel Broken wings and all Waiting for redemption Waiting
to be seen

Did you not hear me I don't exist

But This body
This body lives the day to day Bringing sunshine for all that stay And
Sometimes
Sometimes it freaking haunts me, Taunts me, Makes me

want to scream
Especially when you just sit
and stare
like you don't fucking care
So Through blurred lines
I swallow my bitterness
Walk that front line

with a healing heart
Fueled with passion in exchange for What? pennies? Equality? Respect?
Nothing
After all I don't exist
so Nothing
Nothing except the satisfaction That I am
sun shining
Consistent and strong
bright
A fire that won't burn
And won't leave scars
I might not exist to you
But I am heard
beyond the walls
Beyond the cups of coffee
Beyond the Games, music, laughter and tears
Beyond the hundreds of conversations
My voice still echoes
Reminding me

That I am still standing here For them
and that's what keeps me whole

When I walk through the door where I don't exist

Michele Arcand
Pixelations

We left behind rocks
scattered art
pieces of ourselves
rippling
like the aftermath
of an explosion and time keeps creeping
slowly sifting
handfuls of conflictions
Some serious clouded indecision my pixelated vision
They say Time is reckless
A bandit
That leaves us
In a million tiny pieces
Sleepless
But I say it's beauty
A sunset in July
Where the stars
become our eyes
Shining truths
That offer no hesitation
Truths that offer no Fear
No Regrets
Truths
That remind us war
is child's play
Cause it's a war
Of the ages
That encapsulates us
Leaving us
In cages
But there are no walls
in truths playground
No matter how small
The pixelation

Michele Arcand
Addiction

You puncture my wounds
Till I am bloodless
Like a jellyfish
Yet my heart beats strong
Defining my existence
My total lack of resistance

She plays with my heart
Like a child plays with toys
And I am deep under your spell
Staring in the fire's eye
Till I can't breathe
But
My body craves more
Just a little bit
To ignite my soul
Make me fearless
Keep me Whole
Until I crumble
Once again   Yet

I just want it to stop
But the pain
doesn't even dissipate....
Instead it feels Like a bullet splintering in my back
and I cringe just to breathe it out
and enjoy the colors
that swirl around me
like my dreams.
But her eyes
they burn
like fire
Only feeding her desires
Cause She's got an ache
deep In Her chest
And it don't give me no rest
Cause She just want
one more
Just needs one more
she says I'm flat out

Cray cray
But I know the truth
Is just a shadow
On the needle
That came to save you
Cause she's a little bit ashamed
Just a little bit deranged
By the poison
Running through her veins

And I Just want it to stop
But nothing ever stops
Pain just penetrates
slowly seeping truths
people leave behind

Art by Wayne Burke

Veronica L D
Will There Be Rain

Cradled in the arms of the shores
One body is wading
We are our reflections

Unknowingly disrupted by nature
Molecule by molecule
Slowly... silently... siphoned away

Carried to the heavens
The same, but different
Does it lighten the burden?

Lost particles leave unseen
The mending of pieces,
from crystalline beauty

To all the shades of white to gray
Shouldn't there be warmth,
when roaming so close to the sun?

The distances between,
feel incomplete
Faintly patched together

Deep within the absence and mist
Released to the unsettling
Elements still beating

The wild winds,
are the voice of reason, commanding
Casting, weightlessly astray

As the bodies are waving goodbye
Distorted become the images
Banished from the skies

Sandra Gurney Turner
Lost Expectations

Expectations lost
in a rage of silent passion
Bathe in rawness my love
I reach out my hand to you
A mere token of
words unsaid
with formalities unengaged
I scream to you
in silence
Do you not hear
the thunder
from my heart?
Hold my soul
dearest one
Let it dance with yours
Fear not my tears
for it is not my weakness
that they flow
Let them embellish
your skin familiar
from my bosom
once more

Katie Prior
at last

I slowly memorized the way
you said my first name.
I memorized it like how you
remember music,
by humming along the tune first
then learning the words
and noticing the way each syllable is sung
how it rolls off your tongue.

for the record, I tried
not to fall in love

but at last! slowly slipping southerly
down steep slopes she fell.
there are stories of love I regret,
but none of them started like this.

Benjamin LePage
Growing Up Hastily

Wherever that wind
wanders, will you
too? Into the
oblivion? Oblivious to
demons & treachery?

Graham Groombridge

Weep not as the petals fall,
Nor as the wind blows them away.
One fears the Dogwood's beauty gone,
Yet neither does wisdom fade
Nor saccharine memories sallow.
A new dawn comes,
But sorrow remains,
The soul is fogged in greyscale haze.
Mercifully, the hawk soars to welcome the day,
Right as the sun crests the bay.
Neighborly, the hawk trades place,
That the Owl, his vigil done,
Might rest in light and not in shadow.
Over the bog in watchtower loft,
The Screech owl dreams of Redtail friends
And sunny bays and Dogwood flowers.

(In Memory of Robert Whalen)

Anonymous
Alcoholism

Also known as Alcohol Dependence Syndrome may modify and influence characteristics of one's behavior producing
  a.   momentary emotional enhancement, and
  b.   reduction to anxiety level's that individuals suffering from mood or anxiety disorders may crave. Thus perpetuating patterns of self-destructive behavior.

Causes of Alcoholism include Depression, Anxiety Disorder, PTSD, Genetic Predisposition, and an Overactive Prefrontal Cortex.

Other Causes may include life turmoil, loss, shitty parents, females, loneliness, females, and...
  a.   self-awareness of subtle but gradual decay within one's soul, conditioned by culture, society, and an overstimulated sociological pressure prompted into a state of constant consuming, and
  b.   realizing that we are just manifested consciousness endowed with temporary control of a meat-slop of atoms flying on a giant rock in infinite space.

Excessive Drinking may cause dizziness, shaking, aggression, sexualized compulsive behavior, vomiting, headaches, slurred speech, and...

looking at your bloody fist after a blackout; then looking at your friend on the floor holding the side of his jaw; then watching your friend get up. walk out and slam the front door, shouting, "Fuck you!"

Benefits of Alcohol include

forgetting.

Raymond Foss
Sausage

Forget the frank, the hot dog -
Give me the Fenway sausage.
Lansdowne or Yawkey,
Just give me the street, the crowds, the carts.
Sausage you shrug, you, the reader
Of this trifle, this whimsy -
What do I mean, me the storyteller?
Read on, won't you please.

Peppers and onions
Tease the tongue,
Bun and hot mustard
Set the stage,
The scorched and blackened piece of meat
Reminds me of every one
I have eaten before.

So much memory
Of family and fun
Of ballgames, tailgates, and the carnie;
A cacophony of moments
Drip with grease.
Do you smell it too, sizzling
on the smoky hot grill?

My lips curl with a smirk
Writing these lines
As I laugh to myself
Of the pleasures of excess
And the lusty gluttony
Of eating. . . another one.

Patricia Gomes
Ripening Conditions

There is something
about the pace
of the homeless,
the addicted,
the crazies
walking the early morning streets
when the sun is still low
and muted. Something.
An abrasive irritant
setting your teeth on edge
as you hurriedly pass
those who've no reason to hurry, those
facing long, empty days.
There is something
off-putting
in their five layers of faded clothing,
their outstretched hands, their bag
of discarded cans,
and like an overly-discussed solar eclipse
you cannot,
will not,
must not
look directly at them
because misfortune may damn well be contagious
and not a single one of us
has been inoculated.

Todd R. Nelson
Daddy

With apologies and/or thanks to Sylvia Plath

"You do not do, you do not do
any more," King Coal
of the dead shaft you've forced us
to dig, mining false seams of
hope and lucre, coughing up the bile of
loathing while catching a pure breath
to smile back at you. Daddy,
my canary is dead.

Daddy, the tide gropes your knees,
But you don't know
Your big black toe means
Retreat, take sanctuary
Among your faux trophies
And wives; take the portrait from the mantel,
And drive the hell away.
The planet's warming up—not you.

Go find some cake, or putter by the shore.
Restore "Integrity" to the heraldic lore.
I cannot swim you back
From folly. Stop hectoring
The good and faithful, branding
Loyalty as greatness.

The old world only cedes control
To better men than you.
You want the old world gone,
Not new. You've spoiled that too.
This just will not do.
Consanguinity is taboo.

Your big red tie is way too long;
Your tweets are imbecile and wrong.
You sign your orders with a big bold pen
And think it will impress real men.
You color at the children's table
Hoping for their praise.

I will not testify for you; I've had enough.
Your suitcoat's unbuttoned;
Your grooming's grown tiresome too.
This session's over—
Daddy—so sad—I want to go home—
I'm through.

Ali Gowrie
Cancer

The fog pours like soup across
the highway and I feel lost but
every set of headlights I pass is
my father's blue eyes.

He was always best at navigating
the fog, a red and green light
always finding his way through
the harbors and safely home.

And I cry. I cry for Home. I cry
for him, for his unwavering
strength, for how he has taught me
how to avoid rocks with a blind eye.

Daddy, you have been my
radar, my sail and my wind, my
captain, my anchor and line.
Now let me be yours.

Josh Nicolaisen
Fawning for Something

Pulling on clothes in the blackness of morning,
eating breakfast before my parents wake,
and quietly closing the door behind me-
I've already done this for a few
mornings, and after a couple hours alone,
returned home and off to wait for the bus.

My eyes adjust as I step softly and unsurely,
trying desperately to follow in my father's
footsteps through our field, past the stacks
of cordwood we piled last summer,
and to a stand he built, but was ready
to let his boy sit in.

Through my sights I saw him,
strolling for food at daybreak,
alert and at peace
and with a quick marked movement
I changed that.

Blown backwards, he quivered
in shock, as my shock
caused me to empty
the chamber, missing twice
and sending dirt flying,
while I watched him dying.

After descending my tree
I knelt by his side, stoked his soft
hair, and began to cry.
His breathing slowed until
it was as still as the freshly
fallen snow his body lay upon.

While I rubbed the still-warm fawn
I realized this must have been
his first snow, and that now he'd
never know how his strength would
hold against a New England winter.

Having heard the shots over the
morning's news and carrying his
still-steaming coffee, my father
approached from behind me,
gave me an enthusiastic applause,
teased me a bit over its small stature,
and began to conduct that business
which follows an act like mine,
while I hid my tears, only wiping
them when he'd looked away.

He talked me through what to do
and what to expect but
as I put Grandpa's knife in and
instantly smelled the shot intestine,
the putrid power of the stench
was beyond all expectation.

Slicing anus to breastbone
tearing back skin,
and breaking apart the ribs
so that the steaming organs fell out
staining and melting the snow,
we emptied his insides
to make it even lighter to lug home,
and so my father could teach
me what parts were best to eat.

Stomach turning as I silently
thanked the deer
for his life, our food,
for helping me miss a morning of school,
while for a moment I thought
I felt my father's pride,
but that faded when
I declared I didn't think it was wrong
but that I just couldn't do this again.

Nancy Ferrante
No More

Decaying words and memories

No more sorrows and syllables

Bury them deep within

They don't belong above ground

Or on the surface of my present mind

Crush them like dying leaves

Squashed to pieces underfoot

I am no longer trapped in sad clouds

No longer torn by storms

Decaying words and memories

They will harm me no more

Photo by Julitta Dennison

Tom Driscoll
One Who Climbs Mountains

Frantic emptiness arrived,
aphoristic urgings about the good gone silent
fail their intended effect
in this sea of noise.
Recall how the absurd was once amusing.

Because an image comes to mind again and again—
is it meaningful?

Windswept bare granite— domed rock peak:
my son, as if seated, struggling, inches himself across
the stone, wide eyed in fear the deafening wind
would take him,
                    cast him down.

Years to come we will laugh at the holes worn
in the seat of his pants, my cruel joy watching him,
terror and pride and
 the name he was given that day.

Linda Ohlson Graham
Hush

Hush.
Gusts wade into Ash and Elm woods.
Feathery flakes glean in gilded flurries,
Shimmering, struck by morning star shine.
An elegant waltz in esse, true and bold
Coiling the cogs of the eons eternal.
Blindly forced into holding,
Father Time rusts, usurped.
Clockface mustache crusted with frost
By Old Man Winter's avengement plot.
Pitch pines draped and scrub oaks well dusted,
Take note of the sky, outstretch ancient branches
Compelling roosts to creak and barred owls to yawn.
Tufts of down plunge toward tawny needle duff,
While wood hares leap toward stoic shrub swamps.
Hush.
With orbs rapt and conscience dimmed,
Bearded men stalk alongside lonesome stone walls.
Quiet now, the stag allays all goodly fears of graying days
That prodigious rack the stuff of wagers made for sport
Offset his noble profile, betoken a mortal toll.
While cowled by dawn, good Lady Fate turns her web
Somnolent, her subject, the wise Gully Sage
Plays host to red visions, dreaming of dusky fells.
Hesitant to receive this issuant demand
Spry Sun hangs fire, slow to toll its cosmic tocsin or coruscate
That stags and woodsmen might both decamp, post-haste.
Dancing, dancing, hammer on cap,
Fifth step a prance, sixth step a rout.
From sonorous percussion the winds did jounce!
To one side a broken bolt, the other a fallen crown.
Hush.
A conference ensues between grassblade and dew
Innocent petitions alight, fair Spring Maiden's ears do perk.
"The inevitable is reality, rise now," she did counsel,
"As all beings in you life doth seek," her wisdom incorrupt.
Dictum given, a consensus reached
With dancefloors to polish and seasons to peak
A certain timekeeper's whiskers wiggle
For soon comes the thaw, the rhythm complete.

Rejoicing, rejoicing, at sunshine's behest
Grassblade and dew bury roots once again.
Requests for life granted, Spry Sun oblates
Concedes to his sister, the good Lady Fate
Bright rays a widow's mite to thaw thick granite face.
Hush.
With days of dim gone, on shingles shutters smack
Whistling, awake, housewives dress tables in doilies of lace.
Alas, drifts melted, Father Time jaunts to deliver the news
Of crowns fallen, debts paid and huntsmen run through.
Panting, panting, crags of skin
On shoulders carrying supper, the burden lands.
Trickle, trickle, sweat rolls and blood seeps
Through darkwatch tartan, onerous destiny leaks.
While merry, family bumble and slowly take seats,
Gazing past tankards, bearded smirks abound.
But simpering Kings do halls make dim,
Like fine lancet arches, adorned in icicle shivs.
Hush now, fellow spirit, lest you forget...
The binding of all beings by green and crimson red.

Maya Williams
Shrinking

The inside of my body is shrinking into depths
it never wanted to visit again.

It's difficult to dismiss it as "all in my head,"
when I either feel absolutely everything everywhere
 or absolutely *nothing* everywhere.

It's difficult to believe "it will pass,"
when I'm still in the unbreakable now continuing to shrink.
Continuing to relive a piece of myself that won't disappear,
only this time, I can't "fake it 'til I make it."

It takes more effort to get out of bed
or to do a task than before.

It is not matter of whether I can't
or won't move.
It is a matter of both.

Whether or not writing numbs the pain,
I'll get back to you.

When I say I am shrinking,
instead of the issues *getting* smaller,
I am *feeling* smaller.

When I say I am shrinking,
my screams in my car
and my overcrowded thoughts fighting for space in my mind
aren't making me any bigger.

Not many know that I am shrinking because
I don't want them to know.

After years of teaching myself to be more open about
therapy,
there are still things I don't want people to know.

That is because there are still things I wish I didn't know about myself.

Emily Hall
Lèse-majesté

Dark and mendacious,
eager and seductive,
she pulls me to the trench.
Breath labored, eyes dilated, speech expound the same.
Breaking free from the hold is treason to her constitution.
The crux begins to rev,
and the cravings dethrone.
Before there is sense- its groundless and insatiable rein begins.
Its carnal nature leaves me complacent and hollow.
She breathes deep again,
and my tethered soul follows ready lèse-majesté.

Emily Hall
December Descent

Days of rest, in times of sorrow
Brings birth to a new tomorrow
Light from the earth - arctic sterling
Pulls at our souls – spirits yearning
Days to dread, go to bed
Hibernate until dark is dawn
North birthed to a dark spawn – delicate and unforgiving
Benevolence is near, in fear- run of the mill
Sole sister
– the truth – "sun standing still"

Emily Hall
Until Death

Vows shared at an alter... surrounding her are tears
A beautiful white dress with a clay nose and stiff fingers
Her chariot awaits to bring her to paradise
As the gates of heaven open heads are bowed
As the band slips on...wedding bliss...and cold hands crumble
Until death, until now, embalmed alive for lover's fairy tales
As she kisses the groom the girl she once was slips away
running and laughing through the shadows
The laughing so distant and unfamiliar now and her roses on glossed wood
The tears she tastes and the soil she hears
Wedding bells ring and the cold and brittle bride walks on...

Russell Buker
My Library

I like that
we
can give rise
to
our own creatures

2
cups of dark
coffee
blank-quiet window
to

stare out- coffee
getting
cold after putting
pesky
cat outside to roam

pick
up quick-setting
lime
on dad's trowel
flicking

it onto dense
words
and in between, care-
ful
not to build too

high
during a setting
wanting
to start again
pleading

with son to grind
me
more lime next
time

please and thanks

washing
dad's tools with
milky
water till so
shiny

Julian Collins
Sweet Potato Vine

First, a fist
with dirt and dust
forever trapped
in each crease
bas-relief
edges of sorrow.
Eyes, all sizes
unblinking, vigilante
(inside, sweet flesh:
whispering, chanting
unheard, unseen.)
Then, a glass jar.
Water. A sunny window
Where, propped up,
it takes a long time
you may think
it will never happen
but tiny tendrils
give you feet.
Once rooted,
a dark place is best
but then a green headdress
bursts through your memory.
Vines sprout from your toes
like something forgotten
like something you'd always known.
Leaves unfurl
like cupped hands
they catch your tears
spilling over onto flowers
budding, bursting
blue Calico.
All those years.
All those years you thought
it was the toughness
it was the toughness
that kept you going.

Edward Ahern
Telling a Fortune

Come in, my dear, and sit in that chair.
What's that? No, no crystal ball, no incense.
Just a table, and two chairs, and you and I.
Before you pay me, I must give you a choice.
Choose between two fortunes-neither of them lies.

One lets you look in a mirror,
What you will do, who you will bed,
The future as others are able to see you.
Most are content with that.

The other? Ah, that's much more painful.
I will flay your image and look inside you
At what you become and what you fail to be.
Your essence as it purifies or taints.

Most are unhappy with these revelations,
But recognize their truth
Even though they rarely change.
So which will it be?

Inner or outer, the money is the same.
My actions will not vary.
But I will be looking at you
Either dressed up or naked.

The procedure? Absurdly simple.
Your elbow on the table, fingers straight out.
I set my hands on each side of yours.
And pass them up and down, just not touching.

Your hand feels pressure and warmth.
Both are phantoms but not unreal.
Your focus is through your hand
As I begin to know you.
I ask no questions, that would be fraud.
Only begin to tell you
Of what you will have done
Or what you will become.

What's that? No, of course I understand.
Most people prefer to know
The course of their life rather than
The curses of their nature.
Shall we begin?

Artwork by Joel Carpenter

Jeremiah Camacho
Tomb of the Intimate

I want you
To study
The lore
Of my bones

The tapestry of history
Behind this flesh facade
Peel back my skin
Like a hard cover novel

Unfurl my text
But feel the texture
Of its worth
Along my spine:
First Edition

There are
So many
Words
That
Constitute
My being

But let's start
With
"Ribcage"
Put your hands
Where my lungs should be
And notice the absence
Of breath

If I am, in fact
More than just torso
Perhaps with learned precision
Even you could understand
Why
For generations
It is
That I rattle when I exhale

William Roy

Horse hooves and wax grooves shaped a childhood

Father's hands, well calloused
(His character was well wrought)
Took mine, we crossed some streets
I fell asleep in back seats
Country roads sprint by
Colored with nothin' but fireflies
Beacons in the pitch black
Riding into the moonlight
Toward indifferent mornings
And black coffee

My yard was split-sprinkled
With car parts
And cinder blocks
But we didn't care
"Just never let this end..."
My brother's voice
Whispering to me
As we are both
Engulfed
By sleep

The blue hum of a t.v.
The screech of a faulty turntable needle
And the whinny of a horse
Birdsong nights
Then leaving home flights
Looking back...

Busted shoes and the growin' up blues.

Beth Tremaglio
untitled

Not all who hate each other, know each other

the greatest hatred has grown from desires of reigning over another,
whether the oppressor
or the oppressed.

Not all battles are wars.

Not all wars are about freedom.

Not all but most....

McCaela Prentice
Hellscapes

If there is a Hell
It is as big as the distance between me and you;
As the time between then and now.
It is the same temperature
As the cold sheets on the left side of my bed;
As the mug of hot tea you set down and forgot.

There is nothing but the stiff silence
That followed "I love you",
And the dial tone when you hung up.
It echoes across rooms we never moved into
And rooftop views we never shared.

It's the day I stopped looking for you
And started looking for exits;
It's the one where you don't ask me how my day was,
Or how much longer until I'm home.

It is full of things that never happened,
But should have;
Of things that may never happen,
But could.

It is not for the dead;
It is for the lost,
And so many of them are still alive;
It is proof that nothing is ever totally gone,
Because it is all there
And it is all still out of reach.

Elena Novak
SOMETIMES

Sometimes
I don't even want you
Sometimes
You're a million words behind me
Words I've vomited, breathed, sung, heaved
Words I've pounded on the dashboard
Or smashed upon the table
Or delicately thread through the eye of a needle
But even needles sting
You're a million words behind me
Because you haven't got the time
Too careless and frantic
To breathe the way I do
To feel the way I do
To hear and see and taste the way I do
Sometimes I don't even want you
But I do

Elena Novak
A POEM IN TWO PARTS

I. Meta
Descriptions fall short of a formless entity.
I lost it in a million words about
silly little broken feelings:
It's like ambiguity, shifting shapes;
it's like being pounded by waves.
Other times it's stillness, lying in the dark,
peaceful but ominous with the hidden presence
of a shadow.
It's like drawing a breath cut short,
the antithesis of life.
I walk under the silent blows of an invisible abuser.
The world is a clichéd poem:
unoriginal, stagnant, bullshit.

II. What I Mean to Say
It's like driving down I-75 passing billboard after billboard of senseless
advertisements that
aren't even alluring like "Vote Liberals out in 2010" and "Café Risque: We
Bare All."
I want to drive in peace!

And it comes down hard on you like
A child kneading Play-doh and
She's trying to make you into art but
You come out looking like some misshapen tree
With no leaves because leaves signify life
And life is a word used in platitudes like
"Life is good" or "Life is beautiful"
And you want to believe it so
You think about getting a tattoo that says
"La vita è bella" as a constant reminder but you know
It will stop being meaningful
The same way the first time I moaned but the second and the third and the
fourth time I faked it
And you forget it's even there.
But not this.

Desperate word-vomits like falling rocks obstruct your path and you
Swerve out of the way seeking alternate descriptions but you
Plunge over the cliff and have an out-of-body experience as
You fall.
Reach out and grab yourself.
What I mean to say
Is love.

Elena Novak
CHARLOTTESVILLE

White is the absence of color
that defines whether you end up
at the top of the company or the back
of the police car
White is the absence of understanding
of tiki torches illuminating faces
contorted with hate and fear
Fear of color
Fear of the other
White is the absence of color in a person
murdered by bigotry
and that desolate imagery wasn't enough
to stop the beating, as hearts stopped beating and America was pleading
enough
White is the absence of seeing
that racism is not dead
and we are heading to a place
where not even white is safe
There is no unity in hate
only unity in diversity
and the spectrum of colors
that comprise the human rainbow

Nick Fisk
Idyll

Worn,
but satisfied
by work congruent
to ideals and vocation,
we collapse onto each other
and chatter about critical trivialities.
With your head in lap (or perhaps mine, yours),
we sip freely on the warmth of drinks and laughter
until one nods off, claimed by the other's soft,
and is jolted to by teasing, pointed fingers
accompanied by loving whiny pouts.
Giggles and a playful scuffle
before fresh collapse
both of us happy
and both of us
warm.

Nick Fisk
Astringent

Like fruit
words ripen
carrying their fullest flavor
in a narrow band of instants.
And, like fruit,
words doled prematurely
leave the recipient
with visage twisted
and warped into a
pained spiral,
unfriendly and
unkind.

Likewise,
words nestled too closely
and for far too long
rot and ooze,
their bruised and fetid flesh,
leaving in the mouth of both
maker and consumer,
the unfriendly flavor
called regret.

Still,
despite the bitter twangs
accosting the senses
and
despite the mushy mess
leaving the palate discomposed,
these words
freed too soon
or released too late
unfailingly retain their
indomitable and signature
savor
and
invariably reek of
their knowing essence.

So, do not panic terribly
about the timing of words;
after all,
they
and the people who foster them

Sarah St George
Waterfall Splendor

Standing before waterfall splendor
Close enough to be caressed by her mist
My mind wanders to sweet, sacred places
Gentle kisses, tender embraces
Dreams interrupted by impatient sunrises
Eternal moments ended too soon
Flowing out into distant streams

These peaceful thoughts soon silenced
by the song of the siren in my purse,
The ceaseless ringing,
Obsessive tracking,
Relentless hunting

Hostile echoes from the underworld
Ring through my ear
Remind me of my other life,
My real life,
The one where hellfire is the only source of warmth and light
The life that is my spiritual, emotional, and intellectual death

The soothing sounds of water hitting the rocks
distorted by volcano shrieks,
So much animosity in each syllable,
A half empty milk carton magnified into a missing child,
Full witch burning moon
His tone a black hole sucking me into perpetual despair,
No where to run from the sound of his voice
beginning to sound like my own
Each freckle I was born with just another tracking chip

He will own me until they grow up
This tranquil waterfall, just a hologram projection
A tempting invitation to eternal peace

Sweet Dreams Dad

Dad,
It's hard to believe you have been gone for three years already,
I visit your headstone to pacify mom

but the silence makes me feel more lonely.
I open two cans of beer
One for my shadow
One for your empty chair.

I would like to be able to tell you
That I finally finished school,
I am working as a teacher now
Helping children, putting my love of poetry
to use for something practical.

No more writing elegies for my hopes and dreams,
burning down the world in seventeen syllables
Believe it or not I have actually gotten a few of my pieces published,
not in the Enquirer or in the Prison Poetry Corner.

And yes I left that "Dirt bag"
And the other one...And the other one
I am proud to say that the only abusive relationship I am in is the one
with myself.

My scars have mended into dead end roads
My battered ribcage has become a holding cell for vultures and thieves
but at least my heart is free.

I make my own rules and sorrows,
The house that I am living in was built from the same rusty nails that
gave me tetanus
and brought me closer to Jesus.

I am pleased to tell you that the kids
are doing alright.
John just graduated from kindergarten.
He has taken an interest in dead bugs and excommunicated planets.
Isabel will be going into the second grade.
She twirls around in her tutu majestically.
No, I haven't been able to take them to the beach yet this year
but hopefully I will have more time once my summer vacation arrives,

If I am not buried under a mound of bills and ungraded papers.

I would tell you about the current state of the world, the children in cages,
The war on families,
The war on Happiness,
The war on Life itself
The evil clowns in high places
but that is just too damn depressing and I wouldn't want to re-kill you

So I will just leave you with this:
Sweet dreams Dad. Now is a good time to be sleeping.

Don't worry, your grandchildren are a lot smarter
than me.
I won't let this beer or anymore potential go to waste.

Renuka Raghavan
After the Flames of the Pyre Die Out

We collect the
heaps of ash,
the dry, arid
stench of marrow
blends with the
sweet aromatics of
jasmine and peony.

Our canvas is
the calm river,
a gentle sway
invites us to
her banks on
this bright day.

A Koel
calls out, flying
off to find
a mate.

Soundless intervals
amidst unknown
incantations invoke dead
spirits of our
past to come
and escort the
newest departed soul
to rest.

The fragile staccato of
each spoken hymn
hushes into a
dull beat, a
soft cadence, that
accompanies them to
a quiet place
beyond the blind,
eager reaches of
our longing sorrow.

Renuka Raghavan
Many Little Suns

I lay on the lush green of the Commons watching you traipse through the knee-deep
water of a cement pond, splashing and kicking

each molecule of water momentarily suspended, absorbing the light of day and glowing like
many little suns.

You stand tall, swallowing the clouds, stomping through the river, then the woods veined with
meandering chestnut paths.

This was a place where I could have lain forever, like a resting slug, like a forgotten twig, like an
aging stone.

Steve Whittaker
BY EITHER CIDE

I will die

    In dry fatigue

        Trying to avoid

           Hurting others

                Toward arm-flailing anger
                And eye-obscuring tears

        By dying so suddenly

           By my own trembling hand

Or

        By living too large

           In murmuring, sauntering sullenness

Corralled

    By boisterous expectations

        Of those who claim to care

    I huddle on the inside

        Of an unconcealed, poorly tailored corner

        Least offensive face first

           While despair

             Further defaces and deforms

                My strained shoulders

                  and hunched back

Ian Cappelli
CEMETARIOT

The sparrows sort of rejoice atop the giant stone
crosses. Nobody has a human-sized plastic iPhone
for a grave. I like to think that the sparrows
would enjoy that too.
                          Lichen is the combination
of moss and fungus, and also doesn't really grow
so easily on plastic. It's a product of symbiosis:
the moss part provides the food, the fungus part
consumes the moss part.
                          It would be satisfying if,
instead of any old tombstone, some gravedigger
is hired to hold up my name on a piece of printer
paper like I just flew in from Acapulco.
Only my plane never lands.
                          They're plotting out
where the next coffin will live. Red beetles have
been timesharing in-and-around that area since
the snow melted – they better get a move on.
Someone finished planting the four orange flags.
The pastors are retro
                          fitting that spot for the
construction worker's son with the last name of
"Graves" who died after he plunged into a pool of
molten sap – some especially rural kind of suicide.
An inscription would never tell you that.

Yes, I Would
by Courtney Schlachter, for Scott

Had I met you on the bridge that night,
anticipated your disappointments
before you brought them with you underwater,
I would have caught you-
held you close, tight, wordless,
until your voice warmed the darkness.
You could have told me anything, anytime, all of it,
so I could swallow your words, no matter how heavy
or dirty or grimy with grief,
because I could have buried those too, alongside my own,
instead of burying you.

UNDERGROUND WRITERS ASSOCIATION

Cover Design by Joel Carpenter
Interior Design by Joel Carpenter
Cover Art
Edited by
Volunteer Editors: Valeri Beers

Proof read by: Joel Carpenter
Assistant editor:

Underground Writers Association
Portland, Maine

Support Indie Publishing
facebook.com/undergroundwritersassociation

All rights reserved.
ISBN-13: 978-1727627930
ISBN-10: 1727627938

CPSIA information can be obtained
at www.ICGtesting.com
Printed in the USA
BVHW071133101118
532762BV00018B/458/P

9 781727 627930